Christmas Crock Pot Recipes

Kelly Michaels

Copyright © 2016 Kelly Michaels

All rights reserved.

No part of this book may be reproduced in any form without written permission from the author. Reviewers may quote brief excerpts from the book in reviews.

Disclaimer: No part of this publication may be reproduced or transmitted in any form, mechanical or electronic, including photocopied or recorded, or by any information storage and retrieval system, or transmitted by email without permission in writing or email from the author or publisher.

While attempts have been made to verify all information provided in this publication, neither the author nor the publisher assumes any responsibility for errors, omissions, or contrary interpretations of the subjects discussed.

This book is for entertainment purposes only. The views expressed are those of the author alone and should not be taken as expert instructions or commands. The reader is responsible for his/her own actions.

Adherence to all applicable laws and regulations, including international, federal, state, and local government, or any other jurisdiction is the sole responsibility of the purchaser or reader.

Neither the author nor the publisher assume any responsibility or liability whatsoever on the behalf of the purchaser or reader of these materials.

ISBN-13: 978-1537389059
ISBN-10: 153738905X

"I'm just someone who likes cooking and for whom sharing food is a form of expression."

-Maya Angelou

CONTENTS

Pumpkin Spice Oatmeal 1

Cinnamon Roll Casserole 3

Candied Pecans 5

Monkey Bread 7

Bread Pudding 8

Fudge 9

Pumpkin Pie 10

Sweet Potato Mash 11

Cheddar Creamed Corn 12

Sweet Potato Casserole 13

Butternut Squash 14

Hash Brown Casserole 15

Vegetable Stew 16

Baked Potato Soup 18

Chicken and Dumplings 20

Christmas Ham 22

Cranberry Sauce 23

Stuffing 24

Peppermint Hot Chocolate 25

Creamy Hot Chocolate 26

Sausage Breakfast Casserole	27
French Toast	28
Cinnamon Pecans	29
Apple Crisp	30
Gingerbread Pudding	32
Carrot Cake	33
Christmas Crack	35
Corn Casserole	36
Sweet Potatoes	37
Green Beans and New Potatoes	38
Squash and Apples	39
Crustless Chicken Pot Pie	40
Corn Chowder	41
Turkey Breast	42
Jambalaya	44
Easy Christmas Ham	46
Cranberry Apple Butter	47
Cornbread Dressing	48
Nutella Hot Chocolate	50
Caramel Apple Cider	51
ABOUT THE AUTHOR	53

Pumpkin Spice Oatmeal

Servings: 4

Ingredients:

1 ½ cups milk

1 ½ cups water

1 cup steel cut oats

½ cup maple syrup

¾ cup pumpkin puree

1 ½ tbsp. pumpkin pie spice

½ cup applesauce

1 tsp vanilla

¼ tsp salt

1 cup toasted pecans

Directions:

1. Spray the inside of your crock pot with non-stick spray.
2. Combine all of the ingredients except the toasted pecans in a large bowl and mix together well.
3. Pour the mixture into your crock pot.
4. Cover and cook on low for 4-5 hours.
5. Stir the oatmeal and leave uncovered for 30 minutes to allow it to thicken.

6. Sprinkle the toasted pecans on top before serving.

Cinnamon Roll Casserole

Servings: 6-8

Ingredients:

2 12-oz cans of cinnamon rolls, icing reserved

4 eggs

½ cup whipping cream

3 tbsp maple syrup

2 tsp vanilla

1 tsp cinnamon

¼ tsp nutmeg

Directions:

1. Spray your crock pot with non-stick spray.
2. Unroll the cinnamon rolls from the cans and cut each roll into 4 pieces.
3. Place a layer of the cinnamon roll pieces in the bottom of your crock pot.
4. In a medium bowl, whisk together the eggs, cream, maple syrup, vanilla, cinnamon, and nutmeg.
5. Pour this mixture evenly over the layer of cinnamon roll pieces in the bottom of your crock pot.
6. Place the remaining cinnamon roll pieces in the crock pot and spoon one container of the icing over the rolls.

7. Cover and cook on low for 2-3 hours or until the rolls are set.
8. Drizzle the remaining container of icing over the rolls.
9. Serve warm.

Candied Pecans

Servings: 16

Ingredients:

1 cup sugar

3/4 cup brown sugar

1 1/2 tbsp cinnamon

1 egg white

2 tsp vanilla

4 cups pecans

1/4 cup water

Directions:

1. In a large bowl, mix together the sugar, brown sugar, and cinnamon.
2. In a separate bowl, whisk together the egg white and vanilla until it is a little bit frothy.
3. Spray your crock pot with cooking spray.
4. Put the pecans in the crock pot.
5. Pour the egg mixture over the pecans and stir well.
6. Sprinkle the cinnamon sugar mixture over the pecans and stir well.
7. Cover and cook on low for 3 hours, stirring every 30 minutes.

8. When there are 30 minutes left, pour 1/4 cup water into the crock pot and stuff.
9. Spread the pecans on a baking pan and let them cool for 15-20 minutes.

Monkey Bread

Servings: 10

Ingredients:

1 16-oz roll biscuits

1/2 cup sugar

1/2 cup brown sugar

1 tsp cinnamon

1 stick butter, melted

4 oz cream cheese, cubed and softened

Directions:

1. Spray the inside of your crock pot with non-stick spray.
2. Combine the sugar, brown sugar, and cinnamon in a gallon zip lock bag and set aside.
3. Cut each biscuit into 6 pieces.
4. Dip each biscuit piece into the melted butter.
5. Place dipped biscuits into the gallon zip lock bag with the sugar mixture and shake well to coat.
6. Pour any remaining butter into your crock pot.
7. Transfer all biscuit pieces to your crock pot.
8. Cook on low for 2-3 hours or until dough is done.
9. Stir in cubed cream cheese before serving.

Bread Pudding

Serves: 4-6

Ingredients:

10 slices raisin cinnamon swirl bread, cut into cubes

1 14-oz can sweetened condensed milk

1 cup water

1 tsp vanilla

5 eggs, beaten

Directions:

1. Place the bread cubes into your crock pot.
2. Mix the sweetened condensed milk, water, vanilla, and eggs together in a bowl and pour the mixture over the bread.
3. Stir to coat the bread evenly.
4. Cook on low for 3-4 hours or until set.

Fudge

Servings: 8-10

Ingredients:

1 cup dark chocolate chips

1 cup of coconut milk

1/4 cup of honey

Directions:

1. Mix the ingredients directly into your crock pot.
2. Cook on low for 2 hours.
3. Stir until the mixture is smooth.
4. Pour the fudge mixture into a greased casserole dish.
5. Cover the fudge with plastic wrap and refrigerate for at least 3 hours before serving.

Pumpkin Pie

Servings: 6

Ingredients:

1 15-oz can of pumpkin

2/3 cup cinnamon bun flavored coffee creamer

2 tbsp pumpkin pie spice (divided)

1 9-oz yellow cake mix

1 cup chopped pecans

1/4 cup butter

Directions:

1. Spray the inside of your crock pot with non-stick spray.
2. In a medium bowl, mix together the pumpkin, coffee creamer, and 1 tbsp of pumpkin pie spice.
3. Spread the mixture into your crock pot.
4. In a separate bowl, mix together the cake mix, pecans, and 1 tsp pumpkin pie spice.
5. Sprinkle the mixture over the pumpkin mixture in your crock pot.
6. Drizzle the melted butter over the top of the dry mixture.
7. Cover and cook on high for 2 1/2 hours.
8. Serve warm.

Sweet Potato Mash

Serves: 6-8

Ingredients:

2 lbs sweet potatoes, peeled and chopped

1/2 cup apple juice

1 tbsp ground cinnamon

1 tbsp sugar

1 tbsp brown sugar

1 tsp ground nutmeg

1/2 cup apple juice

1 cup pecans

Directions:

1. Place all of the ingredients except the pecans and the second half cup of apple juice in your crock pot.
2. Cook on low for 4-5 hours or until the potatoes are tender.
3. When potatoes are tender, mash everything in the crock pot with a potato masher.
4. Pour in the second half cup of apple juice and mash more.
5. Top with pecans before serving.

Cheddar Creamed Corn

Serves: 6-8

Ingredients:

32-oz of frozen corn

1 8-oz block of cream cheese, cubed

1 cup shredded cheddar cheese

1/4 cup butter

1/2 cup heavy cream

1/2 tsp salt

1/2 tsp pepper

Directions:

1. Place all of the ingredients in your crock pot and stir well.
2. Cook on low for 3-4 hours or until cream cheese is melted.
3. Stir well and serve.

Sweet Potato Casserole

Serves: 8-10

Ingredients:

2 29-oz cans sweet potatoes, drained

1/2 cup brown sugar

1 tbsp cinnamon

1 stick butter, sliced

1/2 cup heavy cream

1 cup crushed pecans

3 tbsp brown sugar

Directions:

1. Place drained sweet potatoes into slow cooker.
2. Pour in the heavy cream.
3. Sprinkle brown sugar and cinnamon on top.
4. Place butter slices on top.
5. Cook on low for 4 hours.
6. After 4 hours, mash up the sweet potatoes really well and stir everything together.
7. Sprinkle with crushed pecans and brown sugar.
8. Cover and let it cook for another 20-30 minutes before serving.

Butternut Squash

Serves: 2-3

Ingredients:

1 large butternut squash

Directions:

1. Wrap the squash in aluminum foil and cook in your crock pot on high for 4 hours or low for 6 hours.
2. Remove the squash from the aluminum foil and let it cool for 15-20 minutes.
3. Unwrap the squash and slice it in half lengthwise.
4. Scoop the seeds out with a spoon.
5. Scoop the soft squash flesh out of the skin and serve it or place it in an airtight container and refrigerate.

Hash Brown Casserole

Servings: 10-12

Ingredients:

32 oz bag of frozen hash browns

8 oz sour cream

10.5 oz cream of mushroom soup

¼ cup finely chopped onion

2 cups shredded cheddar cheese

½ cup butter, melted

Salt and pepper, to taste

Directions:

1. Slightly break apart the frozen hash browns.
2. Spray your crock pot with non-stick spray.
3. In your crock pot, mix together the hash browns, sour cream, cream of mushroom soup, onion, cheese, and melted butter.
4. Sprinkle the mixture with salt and pepper and cook for 4-5 hours on low.

Vegetable Stew

Serves: 6-8

Ingredients:

2 yellow onions, diced

3 stalks celery, diced

2 large carrots, sliced

3 potatoes, peeled and diced

1 cup mushrooms, cleaned and chopped

1/4 cup lentils

3 cloves garlic, minced

1/2 tsp grated ginger

1/2 tsp thyme

1 bay leaf

2 cups water

1/4 cup soy sauce

Salt and pepper, to taste

Cornstarch

Directions:

1. Place the onions, celery, carrots, potatoes, mushrooms, lentils, garlic, ginger, thyme, bay leaf, water, and soy sauce in your crock pot.
2. Cook for 10-12 hours on low.
3. Around 8-10 hours, add the salt, pepper, and a little bit of corn starch if you want your stew to be thicker.

Baked Potato Soup

Serves: 8-10

Ingredients:

5 lbs russet potatoes, washed and diced

1 yellow onion, diced

5 cloves garlic, minced

2 quarts chicken broth

2 8-oz blocks cream cheese

1 tsp salt

1 tsp bacon

Crumbled bacon

Shredded cheese

Chopped green onion

Directions:

1. Add the potatoes, onion, garlic, chicken broth, and salt to a crock pot.
2. Cook on high for 6-7 hours.
3. Cube and soften the cream cheese and add it to the crock pot.
4. Use a potato masher to mash up the potatoes and cream cheese.

5. Stir well and cook on low for another 2 hours.
6. Top with bacon, cheese, and green onion before serving.

Chicken and Dumplings

Serves: 6-8

Ingredients:

4 skinless chicken thighs

4 skinless chicken drumsticks

1 quart chicken broth

3 cups water

1 small yellow onion, diced

1 stalk celery, chopped

1 tsp dried thyme

1/4 tsp salt

1 12-oz package frozen dumplings

2 tsp butter

1 tsp freshly ground black pepper

Directions:

1. Boil the chicken thighs and drumsticks in chicken broth and water for 45 minutes.
2. Remove the chicken from the liquid and let it cool slightly.
3. Shred the chicken off of the bones.
4. Pour the liquid into the crock pot and set to high.
5. Separate the dumpling strips and break each strip in half.

6. Add the dumplings to the crock pot one at a time.
7. Add the chicken, onion, celery, thyme, salt, butter, and pepper to the crock pot.
8. Let the chicken and dumplings cook on high for 2 hours, stirring occasionally.
9. Reduce heat to low and let cook for another 2-4 hours on low.

Christmas Ham

Serves: 4-6

Ingredients:

1 precooked, spiral cut ham

2 cups brown sugar

1 can pineapple rings

Directions:

1. Sprinkle 1 and 1/2 cups of the brown sugar into the bottom of a slow cooker.
2. Place the ham on top of the brown sugar and pour the pineapple rings and juice on top.
3. Sprinkle the rest of the brown sugar on top of the ham.
4. Cook for 6-8 hours on low.

Cranberry Sauce

Servings: 20

Ingredients:

1 12-oz bag of cranberries

1/4 cup water

3/4 cup orange marmalade

3/4 cup sugar

1/4 tsp cinnamon

Directions:

1. Place all of the ingredients in your crock pot and stir together.
2. Cook on high for 3 hours or until the cranberries begin to burst.
3. Once they begin to burst, gently mash the mixture with a potato masher.

Stuffing

Servings: 14

Ingredients:

12 cups dry bread cubes

4 stalks celery, chopped

1/2 cup chopped fresh parsley

2 tsp dried sage

1/2 tsp dried thyme

1/2 tsp salt

1/4 tsp black pepper

1 3/4 cup chicken broth

1/3 cup butter, melted

Directions:

1. Combine all the ingredients in your crock pot, adding the chicken broth and melted butter last. Mix well.
2. Cook on low for 4-6 hours.

Peppermint Hot Chocolate

Servings: 4-6

Ingredients:

5 cups milk

1/2 cup cocoa powder

1/2 cup sugar

1 cup water

4 tsp peppermint syrup

Directions:

1. Combine the cocoa, sugar, and water in a large pan on your stove. Stir and bring to a gentle boil until the sugar and cocoa are dissolved.
2. Pour the mixture into your crock pot.
3. Add the milk and peppermint syrup to your crock pot and stir.
4. Cook on high for 2 hours or on low for 4 hours.
5. Pour into mugs and serve.

Creamy Hot Chocolate

Servings: 8-10

Ingredients:

14-oz can of sweetened condensed milk

1 1/2 cups heavy whipping cream

6 cups milk

1 1/2 tsp vanilla

2 cups chocolate chips

Directions:

1. Pour all of the ingredients into your crock pot and stir together well.
2. Cover and cook on low for 2 hours, stirring occasionally.
3. Serve topped with marshmallows.

Sausage Breakfast Casserole

Serves: 6-8

Ingredients:

1 lb of cooked ground sausage

12 eggs

1 cup milk

1 1/2 cups shredded cheddar cheese

1 tbsp ground mustard

1 32-oz bag shredded hash browns

Salt and pepper, to taste

Directions:

1. In a large bowl, beat the eggs and add in the milk, salt, pepper, and ground mustard.
2. In your slow cooker, make a layer of sausage, shredded hash browns, and cheese. Repeat the layers once.
3. Pour the egg mixture over the layers.
4. Cook on low for 8 hours (while you sleep!)
5. Top with cheese before serving.

French Toast

Servings: 4-6

Ingredients:

½ loaf of white bread

6 eggs

1 cup milk

1 tsp cinnamon

1 tbsp brown sugar

1 tsp vanilla

Directions:

1. Spray your crock pot with non-stick cooking spray.
2. In a large mixing bowl, whisk together the eggs, milk, cinnamon, brown sugar, and vanilla.
3. Dip each slice of bread into the egg mixture and then place it in your crock pot.
4. Pour any remaining egg mixture on top of the bread in the crock pot.
5. Cook on low 6-8 hours.
6. Serve with fresh fruit, whipped cream, or syrup.

Cinnamon Pecans

Servings: 4-6

Ingredients:

1 1/4 cup sugar

1 1/4 cup brown sugar

2 tbsp cinnamon

1/8 tsp salt

1 egg white

2 tsp vanilla

3 cups pecans

1/4 cup water

Directions:

1. In a large bowl, mix together the sugar, brown sugar, cinnamon, and salt.
2. In a separate bowl, mix together the egg white and vanilla.
3. Add the pecans to the egg mixture and coat them thoroughly.
4. Add the cinnamon mixture to the pecans and stir until they are evenly coated.
5. Pour the pecan mixture into your crockpot and cook on low for 3-4 hours, stirring occasionally.

Apple Crisp

Servings: 4

Ingredients:

5 large apples; peeled, cored, and sliced

1 tsp nutmeg

1 tsp cinnamon

1 tbsp maple syrup

1 tbsp lemon juice

1 cup oats

1/2 cup brown sugar

1/2 cup all-purpose flour

4 tbsp butter

1/4 tsp salt

Directions:

1. Add the sliced apples, half the nutmeg, half the cinnamon, maple syrup, and lemon juice to your crock pot and mix together well.
2. In a mixing bowl, mix together the oats, butter, sugar, flour, the other half the nutmeg, the other half of cinnamon. Spread this mixture over the apples in the crock pot.

3. Cook on low for 4 hours before serving.

Gingerbread Pudding

Servings: 8-10

Ingredients:

1 14-oz package of gingerbread mix

1/2 cup milk

1/2 cup raisins

2 1/4 cups water

1 cup packed brown sugar

3/4 cup butter

Directions:

1. Coat your crock pot with non-stick cooking spray.
2. In a medium bowl, combine the gingerbread mix and milk. Stir in the raisins. Spread the mixture into your crock pot.
3. In a saucepan over medium-high heat, combine the water, brown sugar, and butter. Bring to a boil, reduce heat, and simmer for 5 minutes.
4. Pour the sugar mixture over the batter in the crock pot.
5. Cook for 2 hours.
6. Turn off the crock pot and let it sit for 1 hour without the lid.
7. Serve with vanilla ice cream.

Carrot Cake

Servings: 8-10

Ingredients:

1 cup sugar

2 eggs

1/4 cup water

1/3 cup vegetable oil

1 1/2 cups flour

1 tsp vanilla

1 tsp baking powder

1/2 tsp baking soda

1 tsp cinnamon

1 cup packed grated carrots

Cream cheese frosting

Directions:

1. In a mixing bowl, cream the sugar, eggs, water and oil. Add the flour, vanilla, baking powder, baking soda, and cinnamon. Blend until combined. Stir in the carrots by hand.
2. Spray the inside of your crock pot with non-stick cooking spray.

3. Pour the batter into your crock pot and spread it evenly.
4. Cook for 2-3 hours on low or until a toothpick inserted into the middle comes out clean.
5. Remove the cake from the crock pot, let it cool, and top it with cream cheese frosting.

Christmas Crack

Servings: 10-12

Ingredients:

8 oz unsalted peanuts

8 oz salted peanuts

6 oz semi-sweet chocolate chips

6 oz milk chocolate chips

10 oz peanut butter chips

1 lb white almond bark

Directions:

1. Layer all ingredients in your crock pot, with the peanuts on the bottom.
2. Cover and cook on low for 2 hours.
3. Stir well and let cook for another 30 minutes to 1 hour.
4. Stir again then spoon the mixture onto wax paper or parchment paper.
5. Let cool for at least 1 hour.

Corn Casserole

Serves: 6-8

Ingredients:

8 oz cream cheese, softened

2 eggs, beaten

1/2 cup sugar

8 1/2 oz corn muffin mix

2 1/2 cups frozen corn

16 oz canned cream corn

1 cup milk

2 tbsp butter

1 tsp Cajun seasoning

Salt and pepper, to taste

Directions:

1. In a mixing bowl, combine the cream cheese, egg, and sugar.
2. Mix in the muffin mix, corn, milk, butter, and seasonings.
3. Pour the mixture into the crock pot and cook for 2-4 hours on high.
4. Season with salt and pepper if needed before serving.

Sweet Potatoes

Serves: 4

Ingredients:

4 medium sized sweet potatoes

Butter

Brown sugar

Mini marshmallows

Directions:

1. Scrub, wash, and dry the sweet potatoes.
2. Poke each potato with a fork several times.
3. Wrap each potato in foil twice.
4. Place potatoes in crock pot and cook on high for 4 hours or on low for 8 hours.
5. Top with butter, brown sugar, and mini marshmallows before serving.

Green Beans and New Potatoes

Serves: 6-8

Ingredients:

3 lbs fresh or frozen green beans

4-5 slices bacon, chopped

12 small new potatoes

2 cups chicken broth

1 small yellow onion, diced

1/4 cup butter

Salt and pepper, to taste

Directions:

1. Place all of the ingredients in your crock pot and gently combine.
2. Cook on low for 3-5 hours.

Squash and Apples

Serves: 6-8

Ingredients:

1 ~3-lb butternut squash; peeled, seeded, and cubed

4 apples, cored and chopped

3/4 cup dried cranberries

1 small yellow onion, diced

1 tbsp cinnamon

1 1/2 tsp ground nutmeg

Directions:

1. Combine the squash, apples, cranberries, onion, cinnamon, and nutmeg in your crock pot.
2. Cook on high for 4 hours or until the squash is tender.

Crustless Chicken Pot Pie

Serves: 4-6

Ingredients:

1 can cream of chicken soup

1 can cream of mushroom soup

2 14-oz bags of frozen mixed vegetables

1 tsp oregano

1 tsp dried basil

1 tsp garlic powder

2 cups heavy cream

1 1/2 lbs boneless skinless chicken breasts, chopped

Salt and pepper, to taste

3 cups rice

Directions:

1. Place all of the ingredients in a slow cooker and stir well.
2. Cook on high for 5-6 hours or on low for 8 hours.

Corn Chowder

Serves: 4-6

Ingredients:

16 oz canned whole kernel corn, drained

2 potatoes, peeled and chopped

1 onion, chopped

1/4 cup butter

2 cups milk

2 cups chicken broth

Salt and pepper, to taste

1 tbsp chopped parsley

Directions:

1. Combine all of the ingredients except 1/2 cup of corn, butter, and milk in your crock pot.
2. Cook on low for 7-9 hours, then puree in a blender, food processor, or with an immersion blender and return to the crock pot.
3. Stir in the extra half cup of corn, butter, and milk.
4. Cook on low for another hour before serving.

Turkey Breast

Servings: 18

Ingredients:

3 1/2 lb – 5 lb turkey breast

1/4 cup olive oil

1/2 tsp salt

1/2 tsp pepper

1 tsp garlic powder

1/2 tsp dried parsley

1 large onion, chopped

1 apple, cored and sliced

2 cups chicken broth

Directions:

1. Make sure there aren't any giblets inside the cavity of the turkey breast.
2. Wash and dry the chicken breast.
3. Brush the breast with olive oil and sprinkle on the salt, pepper, garlic powder, and parsley.
4. Place the chopped onion and apple into the turkey's cavity.
5. Place the turkey breast into your greased crock pot, breast side up.

6. Pour the chicken broth over the turkey.
7. Insert a meat thermometer into the thickest part of the turkey breast.
8. Cook for 3-4 hours or until the thermometer reaches 140 degrees F.
9. Cook for another 2-3 hours on low until the thermometer reaches 170 degrees F.
10. Remove the turkey from the crock pot and place it on a roasting pan.
11. Broil the turkey for 5-7 minutes or until the skin has browned.
12. Remove from the oven and let the turkey rest for 15 minutes.
13. Remove the onion and apple from the turkey.
14. Slice the turkey and serve.

Jambalaya

Serves: 6-8

Ingredients:

1 lb boneless skinless chicken breasts

1/2 lb Andouille sausage, diced

1 28-oz can diced tomatoes

1 can rotel tomatoes

1 yellow onion, chopped

1 green bell pepper, chopped

1 stalk celery, chopped

2 cups chicken broth

2 tsp dried oregano

2 tsp Cajun seasoning

2 bay leaves

2 cups white long grain rice

Fresh parsley

Directions:

1. In the crock pot, combine all of the ingredients except the rice and parsley.
2. Cook on low for high for 4 hours.

3. Remove chicken, shred it, and return it to the crock pot.
4. Add rice to the crock pot and stir.
5. Cook on low for 2-4 hours or until rice is cooked. Stir occasionally.
6. Discard the bay leaves and top with parsley before serving.

Easy Christmas Ham

Servings: 10

Ingredients:

7-8 lb spiral cut ham

1 cup brown sugar

1/2 cup maple syrup

2 cups pineapple

Directions:

1. Place the ham inside your crock pot, flat side down.
2. Rub the brown sugar all over the ham.
3. Pour the maple syrup and pineapple over the ham.
4. Cover and cook on low for 4-6 hours, basting the liquid over the ham every hour or so.
5. Remove the ham from the crock pot and let it sit for 15 minutes before cutting and serving.

Cranberry Apple Butter

Servings:

Ingredients:

16-20 apples; peeled, cored, and sliced

12 oz fresh cranberries

3 3/4 cups sugar

1 tbsp cinnamon

1/4 tsp cloves

6-8 pint jars (depending on how big your crock pot is)

Directions:

1. Put the cranberries and apples in your crock pot and turn your crock pot on high.
2. Cook for 18 hours.
3. Add the sugar, cinnamon, and cloves. Stir well and cook for another 4 hours.
4. Spoon the apple butter into the jars, screw on the lids and rings, and let them cool on the counter.

Cornbread Dressing

Servings: 15

Ingredients:

6 cups cornbread

8 slices day old bread

4 eggs

1 onion, chopped

1/2 cup chopped celery

1 1/2 tbsp poultry seasoning

1/2 tsp black pepper

2 10-oz cans cream of chicken soup

1 10-oz cans chicken broth

1/3 cup butter

Salt and pepper, to taste

Directions:

1. Crumble the cornbread and the day old bread.
2. Spray your crock pot with non-stick spray.
3. Add all of the ingredients except the butter, salt, and pepper to your crock pot and stir together.
4. Dot the butter over the dressing and season with salt and pepper.

5. Cover and cook on high for 2 hours or on low for 4 hours.

Nutella Hot Chocolate

Servings: 4-6

Ingredients:

5 cups milk

1/2 cup cocoa powder

1/2 cup Nutella

1/2 cup sugar

1 cup water

Directions:

1. Combine the cocoa, Nutella, sugar, and water in a large pan on your stove. Stir and bring to a gentle boil until the sugar and cocoa are dissolved.
2. Pour the mixture into your crock pot.
3. Add the milk to your crock pot and stir.
4. Cook on high for 2 hours or on low for 4 hours.
5. Pour into mugs and serve.

Caramel Apple Cider

Servings: 12

Ingredients:

12 cups apple juice

6 cinnamon sticks

1/2 cup caramel sauce

Whipped cream

Directions:

1. Place the cinnamon sticks and apple juice in your crock pot and cook for 4 hours on high.

2. Stir in the caramel sauce and serve in mugs topped with whipped cream.

ABOUT THE AUTHOR

Kelly Michaels has been cooking since she could walk. As a child, she would follow her mother around in the kitchen, learning and watching. Her passion has always been food and feeding others. It brings her the most joy in her life. Now she shares her recipes with millions worldwide.

For more recipe books by Kelly Michaels:

Search for "Kelly Michaels Recipes" on Amazon

Printed in Great Britain
by Amazon